# THE
# DUFFER'S
## GUIDE TO
# FOOTBALL

## COLUMBUS BOOKS
### LONDON

Other books in the Duffer's series:

*The Official Duffer's Rules of Golf* (John Noble)
*The Official Duffer's Rules of Tennis* (Bob Adams)
*The Duffer's Guide to Golf: A Second Slice* (Gren)
*The Duffer's Guide to Rugby* (Gren)
*The Duffer's Guide to Greece* (Gren)
*The Duffer's Guide to Spain* (Gren)
*The Duffer's Guide to Coarse Fishing* (Mike Gordon)
*The Duffer's Guide to Cricket* (Gren)
*The Duffer's Guide to Booze* (Gren)
*The Duffer's Guide to Rugby: Yet Another Try* (Gren)
*The Duffer's Guide to Snooker* (Mike Gordon)
*The Duffer's Guide to D-I-Y* (Mike Gordon)
*The Duffer's Guide to Getting Married* (Gren)
*The Duffer's Guide to Skiing* (John Fairbanks)

Copyright © 1986 Gren of the *South Wales Echo*

First published in Great Britain in 1986 by
Columbus Books Limited
19-23 Ludgate Hill, London EC4M 7PD
Reprinted 1987, 1988

Printed by Redwood Burn Limited, Trowbridge, Wiltshire

Typeset by Cylinder Typesetting Limited,
85A Marchmont Street, London WC1N 1AL

ISBN 0 86287 290 1

# CONTENTS

## Introduction

Football goes back to the Middle Ages when peasants used to kick a stuffed pig's-bladder through two sticks — and everyone enjoyed it with the exception of the pig.

Since those early days, the game has developed into the cultured, sophisticated game it is today — arguably the world's greatest game.

However, we at Duffer's Guides realize that there are some who still find certain aspects of the game difficult to grasp — for instance, if the object of the game is to score goals, who invented offside?

So read on, dear reader, and all will be explained.

# Football – Its Aims and Objects

A football match is contested between two teams of eleven players (or as many as you can get on if the opposition is thick and the ref can't count).

The object is, through fair play (or foul play if the ref isn't looking), to kick the ball into the opponent's goal. If this is done without your breaking any of the dozens of laws preventing you from scoring, the referee will blow his little whistle and your team will be credited with a 'goal'.

The game is played during two periods of forty-five minutes, the teams changing ends after the first half. The side scoring the most goals will be considered to have won. Should the scores be equal after ninety minutes, the game is considered to be a draw, and both sides think of it as a moral victory. If one of the sides is from Uruguay, it's an immoral victory.

# Types of Football

Although the basic game of football is fairly well defined through its rules, there are many types of football, each one cunningly different from the other.

## 1. Junior school football

In this type of game the teams consist of any number of players, from four a side to thirty-five plus. In fact, in some of our more over-populated comprehensive schools there have been reports of fifty-three from Form 1A playing sixty-one from 1B.

The beauty of this type of game is watching in amazement how each member of each team, seemingly joined at the shoulders and all kicking at the same time, meanders all over the field before actually managing to score at all.

Duffers, beware. Never agree to referee a junior school football match – it's like having a shoal of piranha around your shins.

## 2. Parks football

Here we see two sides of eleven trying to recreate the hacking, kicking, clogging and ball skills their heroes displayed on the last Match of the Day.

Teams from every trade and profession are involved in parks leagues, and to see building-site labourers kicking accountants or unemployed spot-welders elbowing Inland Revenue clerks is to witness British democracy at its best.

Duffers are advised not too look too interested at a parks match, in case they are asked to play.

### 3. League soccer

This is not to be confused with Football League soccer, which is much posher. League Soccer is, even so, a highly organized game which can be semi-pro or amateur.

The League Soccer teams are usually full of ex-pro players, those hopefuls waiting to be spotted or those who wouldn't play pro-soccer at any price as it would spoil the nice little DHSS fiddle they're on.

Duffers should never buy a used car from a League Soccer type.

## 4.   Football league

The Football League is divided into four divisions and operates on a promotion-and-relegation system. The players are the cream of the nation's football talent. Some can hit the stand roof with either foot from anywhere within the penalty area, while others can fall in the same area, writhing in tackled agony – which promptly ends with the referee clapping and cries of 'Author! Author!'

Teams at the top of the Football League are often watched by sixty thousand fans, while those at the opposite end are watched by a few hundred – mainly relatives.

Duffers should always support at least one Football League club. Unless they do, how do they know which club to hate?

## 5.   Internationals

International matches are battles between the alleged eleven best players from one country playing eleven of the best from another.

Another British pastime, along with trying to fiddle your tax and hating sports commentators, is disagreeing with the national XI, which is selected from the national squad – with which you also disagree, there being at least six players in your club side who are better than 'that bunch of fairies he's selected'.

Duffers should always try to attend International matches. Someone has to.

# The Football Pitch

1. The goal posts – for hitting when faced with open goal.
2. The net – to protect goalie from visiting fans.
3. Penalty area – for falling over in.
4. Penalty spot – for Scots fans to steal.
5. Six-yard box – for goal kicking out.
6. Halfway line – stay behind it, you can't be offside.
7. Centre circle – for kick-off and after goal scored.
8. Corner quadrant – for ball position at corner kicks.
9. The out-of-play line – always claim corner if ball goes over on your attack.
10. The touch line – always scream 'Our ball!' when ball crosses.

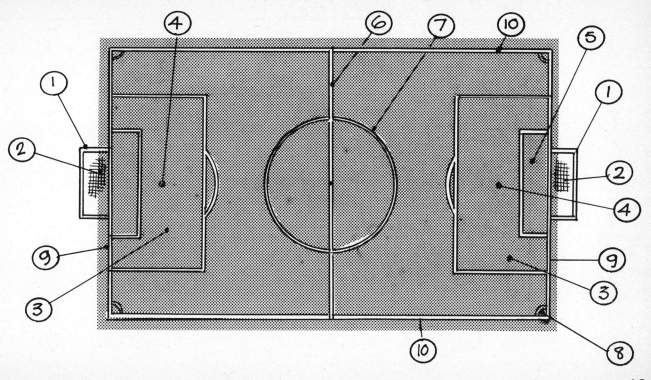

13

## The Players – Who Does What

The eleven players in a team are made up of specialists in certain positions. You, the duffer, should learn to recognize these positions and which players should be doing what. It adds much more of a cutting edge to the insults you hurl from the relative safety of the stand if you know who's failing to do what.

## 1. The goalie

The goalie is the thick-skinned member of the team, taking the blame for everything. He's so unpopular with his teammates that they won't give him one of their pretty shirts to wear. He has to make do with one of another colour. And he's also the only member of the team who doesn't get kissed when they score. That's another strange thing about goalies – they prefer girls.

Duffers can always recognize goalies – they're the ones shouting at their defenders if they actually have to save a shot.

## 2. The sweeper

This player says he's performing behind his defence, sweeping up any ball that they miss. In reality, he's there because he's too slow to catch up his forward-moving defence.

The duffer can always recognize the sweeper. He's the one who's always colliding with his own goalkeeper.

16

### 3. The back four

This type is selected because he can clog, trip and elbow his way to superiority within his own half.

A lovely chap off the field – good to his children and dog (he's even a blood donor) – he can be a pig in the box.

Duffers should always avoid back four types – they carry a government health warning.

## 4. Midfield players

These are usually small chaps whom the soccer commentator refers to as 'midfield dynamos'. It's true, they do run about a lot, but that's only because the opposition psychopath is trying to bring to a premature end the career of these cultured, delicate ball artistes who are trying, unselfishly, to lay on goal-scoring chances for their less intelligent front-runners.

The duffer can always recognize the midfield player; he's the one who is sweating a lot.

## 5.   The striker

He's known variously as the target man and the front-runner, but likes to be called 'striker', seeing himself as a goal-scorer with the speed of greased lightning as he flashes through the gap to crash yet another into the back of the net or to soar high above the opposition defence twenty yards out to power another header into the goal. Actually, he spends most of the game falling over in their penalty area or being offside.

The duffer can easily recognize the striker; he's the one they're all swearing at.

## The Officials

Unfortunately, three officials are required to ensure the game flows smoothly and fairly.

They operate without prejudice, never favouring one player over another – unless, of course, a relative is playing in one of the teams.

## 1. The referee

He is the senior of the officials and his knowledge of the rules is vast. His control over a match is all-important. Weak refereeing will result in an ill-tempered, bruising match with fights breaking out all over the field, whereas strict refereeing will result in a game in which there is no nonsense and a degree of football is played. The duffer is therefore advised to seek out a game refereed by a weak referee if he wants some fun.

## 2.   The linesmen

Linesmen are finks, always telling tales to the referee about sneaky punches going on or the occasional elbow in the ear. They get very excited about offside, too, waving their little flags to let the ref know he's missed the offence.

If the linesman has become a big enough creep and has waved his flag for at least 3,000-plus offsides, he may be promoted to referee and hand in his flag for a whistle. The only visible difference between the two linesmen is that their flags are of a different colour. This is so that the fans can decide which linesman they dislike most.

The duffer can easily recognize the linesmen; they're the ones with non-muddied white socks and even whiter knees.

# Types of Kick

Although the duffer in his early stages of watching or playing football may consider each kick to be the same, this is not so. There are many subtle variations in propelling the ball in the required direction with the foot, and the skilful will be able to use each expertly when required.

## 1. The volley

The volley, or 'on the full', as some commentators prefer to call it, occurs when the ball is met with the foot when it is travelling through the air. The result of this type of shot is often to catch the goalie by surprise, when he was expecting the ball to be blasted at him instead of flattening the corner flag.

## 2.  The half volley

In this shot the ball is kicked as it rises from the ground and, as may be guessed from its name, only half-flattens the corner flag.

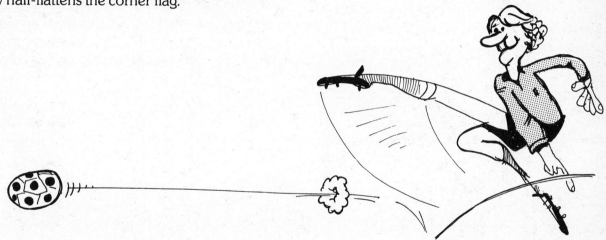

### 3. The mis-kick

This particularly devious skill can often throw a whole defence – who, doubled up with laughter at your total incompetence, fail to see the team-mate behind you smack it into the back of the net from fully thirty yards.

You, of course, being the sportsman you are, claim you were playing a dummy.

## 4. Long floated cross

Use this ball from the touchline to the far post when you can't think of anything constructive to do, or when a big, nasty defender (who looks as if there could be a bit of Uruguayan blood there somewhere) comes anywhere near you.

## 5.  Swerve shot

This shot is beloved by Brazilians, who spend a lot of time bending their balls. The skill of this kick is to hit the ball slightly off-centre with either the inside or the outside of the boot, thus giving a spin effect which causes the ball to swerve left or right.

This is often used from a free-kick situation to deceive a goalkeeper, who is amazed to see the ball curve ten yards past his upright while a straight drive would have ended up in the back of the net.

### 6. The back flick

Sometimes known as the back heel or the surrender ball, it is used by cowards everywhere who are confronted by a big, hairy tackler – in preference to nobly sustaining a smashed tib and fib. The ball is back flicked and, with hands held aloft and cries of 'I haven't got it', he lives to strike another day.

### 7. The delicate chip

You must only use this when you're fairly certain the TV cameras have you in close-up. The ball is delicately pushed out of picture (anywhere will do just as long as it looks good). You will soon be considered by TV soccer fans to be a stylish creator. They're not to know that out of picture it's the third scoring pass that afternoon you've given to a linesman.

30

## 8. The bicycle kick

This very exciting yet flashy kick is used by the team extrovert when, with back to the goal, he takes off vertically in the hope of meeting a high cross, sending it into the goal.

This shot is also popular with goalies because it hardly ever goes under bar height, and osteopaths who make a fortune out of attending to disc problems on players who perform this shot. One Liverpool player so perfected the bicycle kick that he could ruin a Raleigh in forty-five seconds.

# Referees' Signals

The referee, as you probably know, is the little chap dressed in black who keeps blowing his whistle and generally tries to ruin the game by stopping fights and disallowing offside goals.

To help the referee there is a series of signals he may use to indicate to players and spectators why he has made certain decisions.

These signals are, of course, understood by the regular player or supporter, but for the duffer, who may be a trifle confused by the ref's arm-waving, the following explanations may came in useful.

My guide dog has
bitten me.

I don't know what
it was but something
illegal must have
happened there.

Their psychopath
just gave me the
evil eye.

33

Look,
there's Concorde.

Blast those
curried eggs.

I'm booking him
for diving.

34

I'm going to see
Nureyev tonight.

My son wasn't
offside then.

I've just swallowed
my whistle.

35

My sciatica is
playing up again.

My auntie is
in the stand.

Shhh – the goalie's
asleep.

36

I shouldn't have
had that bottle of
gin at half-time.

I'm turning right.

37

# Are You Cut Out to Be a Football Fan?

Many people find out too late that they are not suited to being soccer fans, so before you, the duffer, make any decisions in that direction, let the following questionnaire provide you with a guide as to your suitability.

**1.  Do you want to be a soccer fan because:**

(a)  It gets you away from the wife?

(b)  It gets you away from the wife and kids?

(c)  You enjoy swearing in public?

39

**2.  When a player from your side misses an open goal, do you:**

(a)  Shout, 'Hard luck, old chap'?
(b)  Throw your pastie at him?
(c)  Run on the field and strangle him?

**3.  In a Cup semi-final, the ref awards a last-minute penalty against your side. Do you:**

(a)  Accept the decision with grace?

(b)  Generously proffer the name of a good optician?

(c)  Write poison-pen letters to his wife?

41

**4. Can you honestly say:**

(a) I don't care who wins as long as it's a good game?

(b) I don't care who wins as long it's a fair result?

(c) I don't care who wins as long as it's us?

42

**5. Do you support your team:**

(a) Because their shirts are a pretty colour?

(b) Because you admire their style of play?

(c) Because you like the beer that's on at the club bar?

**6.  Would you travel away to support your team on your wedding anniversary?**

(a)  No, certainly not.

(b)  Only if you were back in time to take the wife out for dinner.

(c)  Only if you could stay away for the night with the boys.

44

**7.    The linesman's raised flag has robbed your side of a match-winning goal. Would you:**

(a)  Graciously point out the error of his judgement?

(b)  Comment on his parentage?

(c)  Stuff his flag down his earhole?

**8.   A visiting fan has offered the opinion that your team's captain is a loud-mouthed psychopath. Do you:**

(a)  Offer to debate the point over a medium dry sherry?
(b)  Ignore his criticism?
(c)  Plant your wallet on him and report him to the police for pickpocketing?

Score 1 for each (a); 2 for each (b); 3 for each (c).

0 – 9      Perhaps you should try flower-arranging.
10 – 17  Could try harder.
18 – 24  Congrats, you're club manager material.

# How to Play Dirty

You, the innocent duffer, may decide you'd actually like to play the game. There are many courses available through which your natural talent can be encouraged and developed.

What these courses don't teach, however, are the dirty little tricks that are so important to any self-respecting player.

We at Duffer's Guides, nothing if not thorough, urge you to practise the following ploys, initially in the privacy of your own home before you unleash yourself on your unsuspecting opponent.

## 1. The classic (Uruguayan) over-the-top

Use this only in case of dire emergency (if you are playing against your local VAT man, for example). The object is to look as if you are challenging for a 50–50 ball, but you innocently put the sole of your boot over-the-top of the ball, making contact with his shin just as he's making contact with his boot.

Be very careful using this ploy because the sound of cracking you will hear can often be very upsetting.

## 2. The wall ploy

When the opposition are lining up to block a free kick, they form what is called a wall. The players in this wall are always far too busy protecting their tender naughty bits to notice you on your hands and knees behind them tying all their boot laces together.

The beauty and grace of this ploy will not become evident until the players in the wall try to break in different directions.

### 3. Unnerve-the-sweeper ploy

To use this ploy at its most effective you should gain the confidence of the opposition striker, then casually make a remark something like 'How's your lovely wife – is she still sleeping with our goalie?'

He'll then spend so much time in your penalty area, trying to kick your goalie, there'll be no one at the back of their defence to stop you making a great name for yourself.

## 4. The sporting gesture ploy

There are two classic versions of this ploy. In the first, you offer a helping hand to lift up the opponent you've just flattened. This gesture of goodwill will change the mind of the ref who was about to book you. What he does not see is the spiked strap you have in the palm of your hand with which you crush and stab your opponent's hand.

For the second version, you wait until your opponent has just missed scoring what would have been a lovely goal. To show your appreciation, you run over to him as he sits on the turf, reflecting on his near-miss, and sportingly tousle his hair in a gesture of sympathy.

What your admiring fans don't see is that you're also pulling lumps of his hair out – and revelling in his screams of agony.

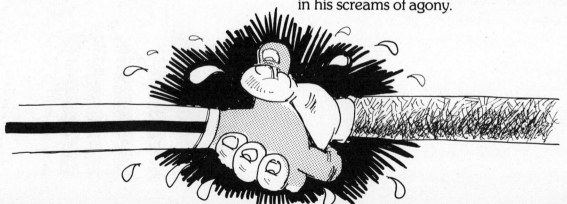

## 5. Be a ventriloquist

This is the most beautiful of all the ploys. It almost makes dirty play an art form, and it can be used in all parts of the field. For instance, in their penalty area, you completely confuse the opposition's goalie who is coming out for a high ball with no teammate near him. Throwing your voice, you say, 'O.K., Fred, let it come.' He does and it lands at your feet and you bang it in.

Another variation on this theme is to throw your voice in the direction of the opposing players and say, 'Ref, you're a useless !!XX**.' When the demands to know who said that, you offer the name of their star player – again by throwing your voice – and he gets sent off.

# Bluff Your Way Through Soccer Chat

Most duffers feel, being new to the game, rather self-conscious about joining in soccer chat.

There is, of course, no need to feel inhibited now that you are the proud owner of this *Duffer's Guide to Football*. With close attention to what follows, and just a few hours of time and effort, you can turn yourself into a force to be reckoned with when it comes to football chit-chat.

One word of warning, don't overdo the pontificating — after all, you don't want to become a TV pundit, do you?

Substituting him for Jones would have given the attack greater width.

If only he'd hold the ball a fraction longer, allowing his overlap player positional superiority.

He's got his angles all wrong there.

He knows the situation calls for a 4-2-4 and he continues to play 4-3-3!

54

Their right side was exposed to direct supported running.

Remember Pele did that in '74?

Couldn't they see he was weak going left?

It's obvious to everyone — their midfield man was
unable to read the options.

Frankly, I doubt he's got the on-the-ball vision.

He misses the freedom of a more lateral attack.

## I Play Soccer Because . . .

The soccer duffer must not believe that love of the game has anything to do with why people play it. Go on, ask any teammember to give you an honest answer to 'Why do you play soccer?' None of the answers has anything to do with sporting confrontation.

1. I just adore dressing up.

2. I hate the game – but it gets me away from the wife.

3. I love inflicting pain on complete strangers.

4. I'm trying to get even with that goalie who ran off with my bird.

5. I love kissing whoever scores — even the
   opposition sometimes.

62

6.  I enjoy being in the showers with the boys.

63

7. I hate the game – I enjoy the booze-up
   afterwards.

# Understanding the Commentator

During the extensive market research carried out in preparation for *The Duffer's Guide to Football*, we asked five thousand duffers which was the most difficult aspect of football to understand. The vast majority said 'understanding the commentator'. The vast minority said, 'Mind your own bleedin' business, you nosey sod!'

Here, at no additional cost, we offer a guide to what the commentator really means. After all he, unlike us folk on the terraces, cannot indulge in the pure joy of screaming insults at the players.

**He's playing with great belief in himself.**
He's a greedy little sod.

**He knows what's expected of him and he's out there trying to do it.**
He's the team thug.

**He's the team motivator.**
He's the team big-mouth.

**He plays with total commitment.**
He only knows one tactic.

**He's been just everywhere
this afternoon.**
Offside . . . given a penalty
away . . . fell over the linesman . . .

**He's tipped to become
an International player.**
. . . by his mother.

**He's always doing the
unexpected.**
He mis-kicks a lot.

**He never knows when
he's beaten.**
He should have packed it in
years ago.

**He's very positive in the tackle.**
He goes for the knee-caps.

**He's very quick off the mark.**
He's offside most of the time.

**I'm surprised to see him included in the team today.**
I thought he was still inside.

**He goes for anything in the air.**
When the ball's on the ground, he's rubbish.

**His pace is very deceptive.**
I didn't know he was as
slow as that.

**I think he's a player
of great talent and promise.**
He's slipped me twenty
quid again.

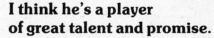

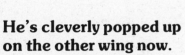

**He's cleverly popped up
on the other wing now.**
The clown! He's got no
positional sense.

**His contribution often
goes without notice.**
He does very little.

**He plays with equal ability up front, midfield or at the back.**
He's rubbish everywhere.

**He's made the position virtually his own.**
He's broken his deputy's leg.

**He's a very underrated player.**
So he tells me.

**The ref's interpretation of the rules is interesting.**
I haven't got a clue what the ref is doing.

## *Football Songs*

Just because you are new to the game, you must not feel left out of being part of the popular bank choral society.

To save you the trouble of learning all the complicated words, you will find printed on the following pages the words of those songs football fans love so well. Just cut out the pages and take them with you when you next attend a game.

Don't worry too much about learning the tunes. They don't really matter.

## 1.  Here We Go

1.  Here we go, here we go, here we go.
Here we go, here we go, here we go-ow,
Here we go, here we go, here we go,
Here we go-ow, here we go.

2.  Here we go, here we go, here we go.
Here we go, here we go, here we go-ow,
Here we go, here we go, here we go,
Here we go-ow, here we go.

3.  Here we go, here we go, here we go.
Here we go, here we go, here we go-ow,
Here we go, here we go, here we go,
Here we go-ow, here we go.

Try your best to memorize the words as soon as
you possibly can.

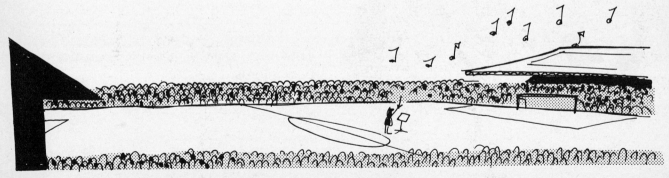

**2.  One Nil** (tune: 'Amazing Grace – She Was a Liverpool Girl', arranged Thug & Clog)

One nil, one nil
One nil, one nil
One nil, one nil
One nil.
One nil, one nil
One nil, one nil
One nil, one nil
One nil.

There are slight variations, of course, on the basic words...

If your team should become two-nil up, the song becomes:

Two nil, two nil
Two nil, two nil
Two nil, two nil, etc.

This change may seem difficult at first but, with concentration, you will find you'll probably be able to master it.

74

# The Manager

Soccer teams, no matter how humble or how great, must have a manager. After all, no matter how useless the team, someone else has to take the blame. However, when things go well, the team takes the credit — so you have to be a very special sort of person to be a manager: a dedicated masochist who loves the game.

1. Rose-coloured spectacles
2. Thick skin
3. Iron fist in velvet glove
4. Great vision
5. Voice – a whisper should carry 150 yards
6. Track suit – looks as if you're earning your keep
7. Boots or trainers – if you wear wellies, they think you're the groundsman
8. Hat – the odder the better
9. Sick parrot – for comparison
10. Transfer forms at the ready, in case you find a Maradona going for 50 quid
11. Chewing-gum – don't know why, but it's compulsory
12. Springs in boots for leaping up and down from bench
13. Numb bum from sitting on damp dug-out benches
14. Always show some sports firm's trademark – encourage the freebies

# Soccerspeak

Many people like to perpetuate the mystique of their profession by cloaking it in a language which can be understood only by another of the same profession. The medical and legal worlds are good examples.

Football, too, has a language all its own, understood only by players, who use it on after-match interviews.

Haven't you ever wondered what the flame-haired midfield dynamo was talking about? Well, you're about to find out.

**At the end of the day, it's all about goals, Brian.**
If we score more than them, we win.

**At the end of the day, it's eleven of them against eleven of us, Brian.**
And if our eleven can clog them first, we're in with a chance.

**The boss.**
The manager.

**Billo gave it to Daveo who slotted it to Charlieo who stuck it into the box an' I got on the end of it, Brian.**
The ball came to me via William, David and Charles and I scored.

**I nutmegged him.**
I pushed the ball through his legs and ran around him.

78

**It was all about teamwork, Brian. I just happened to be there to nod it in.**
I got there faster than anyone else.

**We were all working for each other, Brian.**
We were all trying to be glory boys.

**I'm over the moon, Brian.**
I'm absolutely delighted.

**I'm gutted, Brian.**
I'm terribly distraught.

**I'm sick as a parrot, Brian.**
I'm gutted.

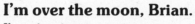

JUST BETWEEN THE TWO OF US - BRIAN...

HOW TO SPEAK JIMMY HILLEEZE

79

**If we get a result . . .**
If we win . . .

**We didn't get a result.**
We didn't win.

**I turned him inside out.**
I dribbled around him.

**The cup's a great
leveller, Brian.**
I'll have him on his back
within five minutes.

**Knockout, mate.**
Very good, my friend.

**Magic.**
You did that rather well.

80